Acc 4514.

This book is to be returned on or before the last date stamped below.

ANDREW MARVELL
SCHOOL LIBRARY
PLEASE RETURN

ANDREW MARVELL
SCHOOL LIBRARY
PLEASE RETURN

A Century of Change

Health and Medicine

Jane Shuter

Heinemann
LIBRARY

First published in Great Britain by Heinemann Library,
Halley Court, Jordan Hill, Oxford OX2 8EJ
a division of Reed Educational and Professional
Publishing Ltd.
Heinemann is a registered trademark of Reed Educational
& Professional Publishing Ltd.

OXFORD MELBOURNE AUCKLAND
JOHANNESBURG BLANTYRE GABORONE
IBADAN PORTSMOUTH (NH) USA CHICAGO

© Reed Educational and Professional Publishing Ltd 1999
The moral right of the proprietor has been asserted.

All rights reserved. No part of this publication may be reproduced, stored in a retrieval system, or transmitted in any form or by any means, electronic, mechanical, photocopying, recording, or otherwise without either the prior written permission of the Publishers or a licence permitting restricted copying in the United Kingdom issued by the Copyright Licensing Agency Ltd, 90 Tottenham Court Road, London W1P 0LP.

Designed by Celia Floyd
Originated by Ambassador
Printed in Hong Kong/China

03 02 01 00 99
10 9 8 7 6 5 4 3 2 1

ISBN 0 431 03879 1

British Library Cataloguing in Publication Data

Shuter, Jane
  Health and medicine. – (A century of change)
  1. Medicine – Great Britain – History – 19th
     century – Juvenile literature
  2. Medicine – Great Britain – History – 20th
     century – Juvenile literature
  3. Health – History – 19th century – Juvenile
     literature
  4. Health – History – 20th Century – Juvenile
     literature
  I. Title
  610.9'41'09034

Acknowledgements
The Publishers would like to thank the following for permission to reproduce photographs:

Corbis, pp. 8, 9; Jeff Moore, p. 25; Mary Evans Picture Library, pp. 10, 21, 22, 24, 26; Science Photo Library, pp. 5, 7, 11, 13, 15, 19, 20, 27, 28, 29; The Salvation Army, p. 4; Tony Stone Images, p. 17; Wellcome Institute Library London, pp. 6, 12, 14.

Cover photograph reproduced with permission of Science and Society Picture Library and Science Photo Library

Our thanks to Becky Vickers for her help in the preparation of this book.

Every effort has been made to contact copyright holders of any material reproduced in this book. Any omissions will be rectified in subsequent printings if notice is given to the Publisher.

For more information about Heinemann Library books, or to order, please telephone +44 (0)1865 888066, or send a fax to +44 (0)1865 314091. You can visit our website at www.heinemann.co.uk

Any words appearing in the text in bold, **like this**, are explained in the glossary.

CONTENTS

Introduction	4
Seeing the doctor	6
Nurses	8
Diagnosis	10
Hospitals	12
Pain relief	14
Surgery	16
Killer diseases	18
Medicine	20
Alternative medicine	24
The future?	28
Glossary	30
Index	32

INTRODUCTION 1900

Medical care in 1900

Most people in 1900 were unlikely to see the doctor unless they were very ill. There was no system for giving babies checkups or older children **vaccinations**. People had to pay to see a doctor. If they needed medicine, then they had to pay for that as well. Many people just could not afford this. A visit from the doctor and a single **prescription** for medicine cost about five per cent of a worker's weekly wage, and it could cost far more. Workers hardly ever had this much money left over from their wages after rent and bills were paid.

Different kinds of care

The kinds of medical care available depended on where you lived and how rich you were. In some areas, especially big cities, nurses visited ordinary people in their homes and gave free advice on keeping healthy and caring for the sick. They were paid for mostly by charities. Some hospitals provided free emergency care for the poor. But in rural areas, especially remote places, people had to rely on the help of local people who had basic medical skills.

As good as it gets

In 1900 even the most up-to-date medical treatment was mainly concerned with easing pain and not curing disease. Doctors could set broken limbs and extract painful teeth. Any other forms of treatment were mostly based on common sense and previous experience. Doctors varied widely in their level of skills, although to be a doctor you had to pass a basic four-year training course.

In the early 1900s most poor people never saw a doctor. They were more likely to get advice from nurses and midwives who made home visits, like these in London's East End.

2000

Modern medical care

Now, most people who live in **developed countries** go to the doctor regularly. There are many more treatments and medicines available for when they are ill.

Kinds of care

The kind of medical care you get still varies. There are more machines that can **diagnose** diseases and more medicines for treating patients. People are given **antibiotics** to fight wound infections which would previously have killed them. Antibiotics are also used against other infections that are painful rather than deadly, such as throat and ear infections.

In the UK there are two systems of health care. The National Health Service (NHS) was set up in 1948 to provide free health care for everyone. Everyone who works pays for it with some money from their wages. Today, patients have to pay for prescriptions and some treatments as well. But the NHS is still cheaper than the private medical system which runs alongside it. In 1997 a private patient could pay about £500 to have a gall bladder removed, after a wait of a few weeks. A NHS patient would not have to pay.

A waiting room in a modern doctor's surgery.

But they would have to be on a waiting list for more than a year before the operation.

A new age - again

There is a big difference between the medical care available in 1900 and modern medical care today. Yet at both times there have been medical advances to make people very hopeful about the future. In 1900, increased standards of **hygiene** and the discovery of vaccines for many **contagious** diseases had dramatically lowered the death rate. Modern medicine has been looking at **DNA** and **gene** replacement to provide cures for many diseases.

SEEING THE DOCTOR   1 9 0 0

Where?
In 1900 doctors did not usually have offices or surgeries. They visited people in their homes or, if things were really serious, in hospital. Either way, people usually had to pay to see the doctor. In some towns and cities in the **developed countries** poor people were seen for free in hospitals set up by governments or charities, such as the Salvation Army.

When?
Even well-off people did not call the doctor in very often. They would not have seen a doctor for colds, infections, sore throats or even childhood diseases such as mumps and measles. There would have been nothing that the doctor could have prescribed anyway. Instead, people relied on traditional remedies, like cloves for toothache or a roast onion held to the ear for earache. Doctors were a last resort, called in when the patient was seen as seriously ill.

How much?
The cost of calling in a doctor and the price of any prescribed medicines varied from country to country and from doctor to doctor. Some doctors who lived in the big cites only treated the rich and so charged a lot of money – as much as an ordinary worker's yearly wage. Other doctors who worked in rural areas, mostly with poor families, often accepted food or livestock as payment.

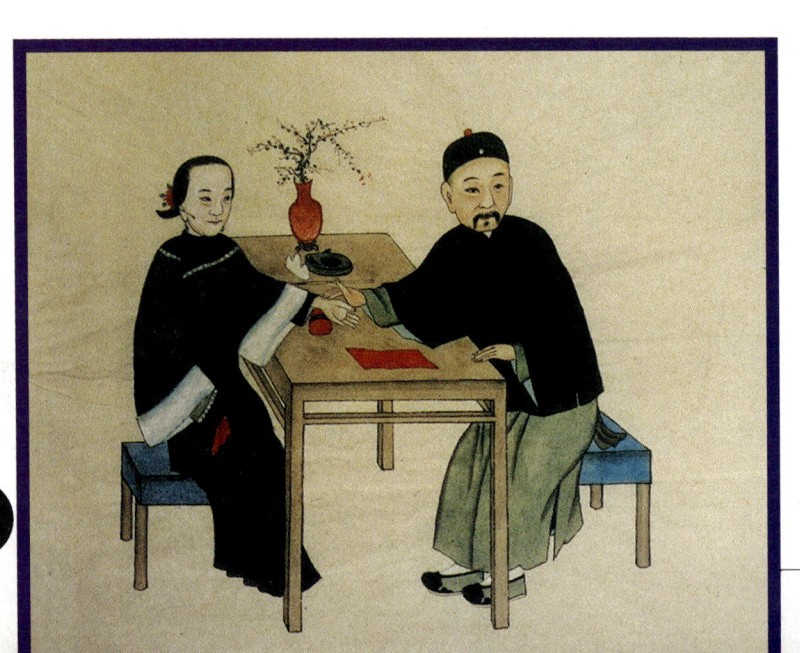

Chinese doctors had to have qualifications long before doctors in Western countries such as the UK. Some were paid all the time that their patients were well, as a reward for keeping them well. Patients stopped paying them any time they became ill!

2000

Where do people see the doctor now?

People now visit the doctor at clinics, health centres or surgeries. In emergencies they go straight to the hospital. Doctors only call on people at home if they are too ill to reach the surgery, but not ill enough to go to the hospital.

What can be treated?

Most people now expect to feel well most of the time. They often go to the doctor as soon as they start to feel ill because they know that doctors have a wide range of medicines, tests and treatments. Doctors now have treatments for many minor ailments that they would not have had medicines for in 1900, such as **antibiotics** for infections. They also provide services that were not available in 1900, such as checks for diseases like breast cancer.

What does it cost?

The cost of calling a doctor in, and the cost of any prescribed medicine, still varies from country to country. Some countries provide free health care for everyone. Some countries charge everyone for health care. Some countries charge some people and not others. Even where people are charged for health care, the cost is rarely as large a part of their wages as it was in 1900.

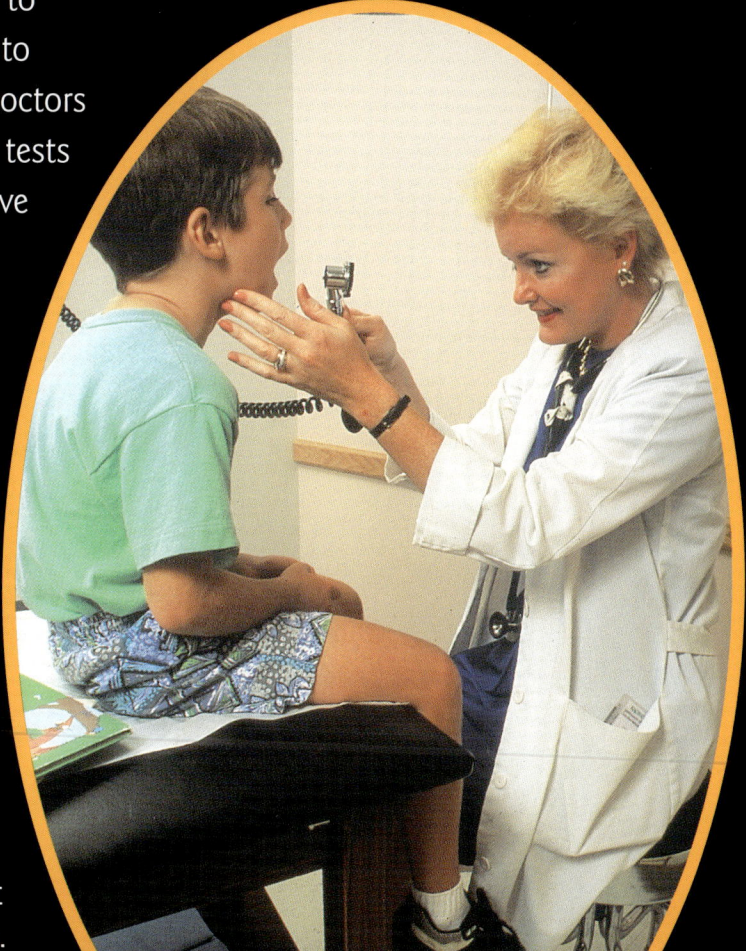

This doctor is using a light to examine a boy's throat. The light shines into and magnifies the back of his throat making it easier for the doctor to see any infections.

NURSES

1900

A new profession

In 1850 anyone could become a nurse. There was no training and nurses were either badly paid or not paid at all. By 1900, nursing was a recognized profession. People could train to be a nurse and nurses had more responsible jobs; for example, they gave medicine and treated wounds. They also helped in operations, from taking out tonsils to amputating limbs.

By 1900, there were over 64,000 trained nurses in Britain alone. But there were still places in the world without trained nurses – both in **developing countries** and in rural areas of **developed countries**.

The recommended time for nurse training in the UK was three years, but training was not enforced by law until 1919.

Florence Nightingale

Florence Nightingale (1820-1910) helped to change nursing practice and how people thought about nurses. She helped nurse the sick during the Crimean War (1854–6). She and her nurses cleaned up the filthy wards and washed and cared for the patients. The improved **hygiene** made the death rate in their hospital at Scutari fall by 40 per cent.

As part of their training, nursing students had to watch operations. This photo was taken in St Luke's Hospital, New York, in the 1890s.

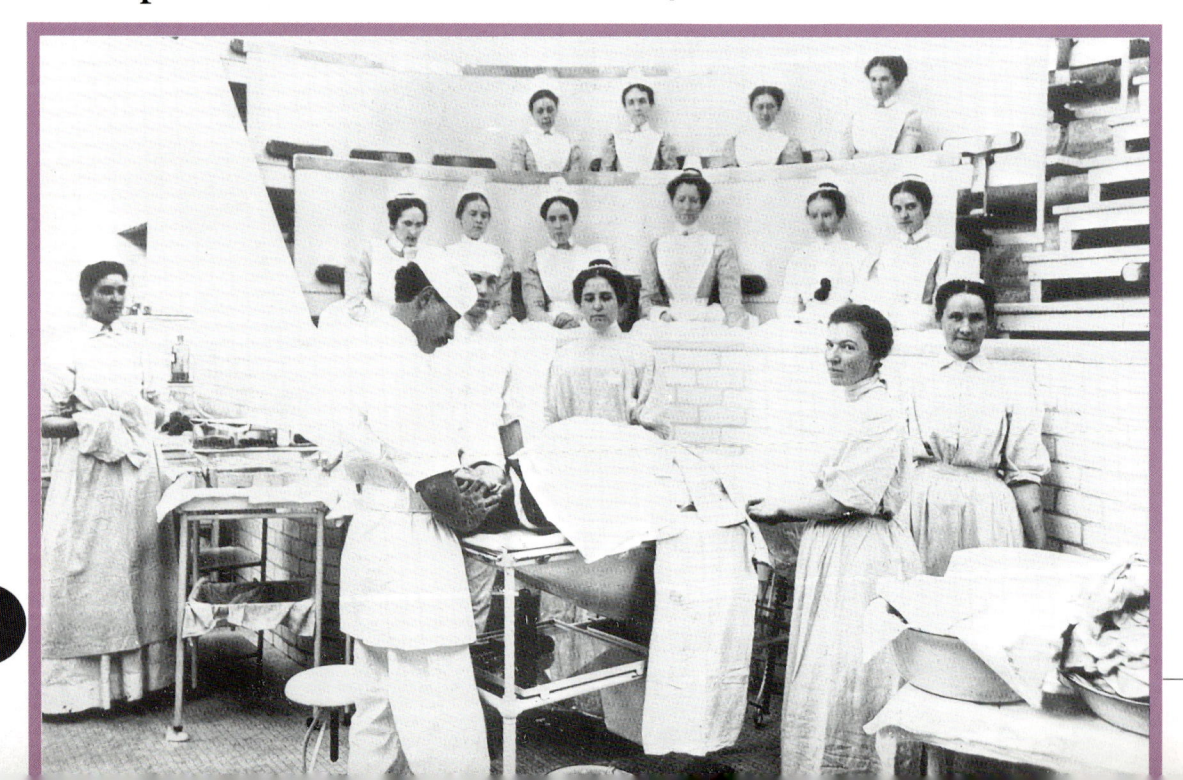

2000

Modern nursing

Today, women and men must spend just over three years in nursing colleges and pass examinations to qualify as nurses. As students they work in hospitals and clinics, gaining practical experience in several sorts of nursing. They have to learn **anatomy**. They learn about drugs and medical procedures, such as feeding unconscious patients through a tube. They also learn how to deal with medical emergencies, from heart attacks to severe burns.

Specialization

Most nurses now **specialize** in one kind of nursing. This means they go on to do a year or more of extra training after they qualify as general nurses. Some of them work as **midwives**, caring for pregnant women and their babies before, during and after the birth. Others work in the accident and emergency ward of hospitals, or specialize in caring for patients with heart problems.

Male nurses

In 1900 nursing was seen as a job for women. Men either became doctors or orderlies – men who did the heavy work, the fetching, lifting, carrying and cleaning. Women did the 'caring' part of the job. But attitudes changed, especially as a result of the nursing work done by men in the wars fought since 1900. Now more and more men are training as nurses, and are accepted as such by patients and the rest of the medical profession.

Nurses now have to be able to use a lot of complicated equipment to care for their patients. This baby would have died had it been born in 1900. The baby is hooked up to a machine that keeps its heart beating, and is fed through tubes. Modern machinery and modern nursing are keeping the baby alive.

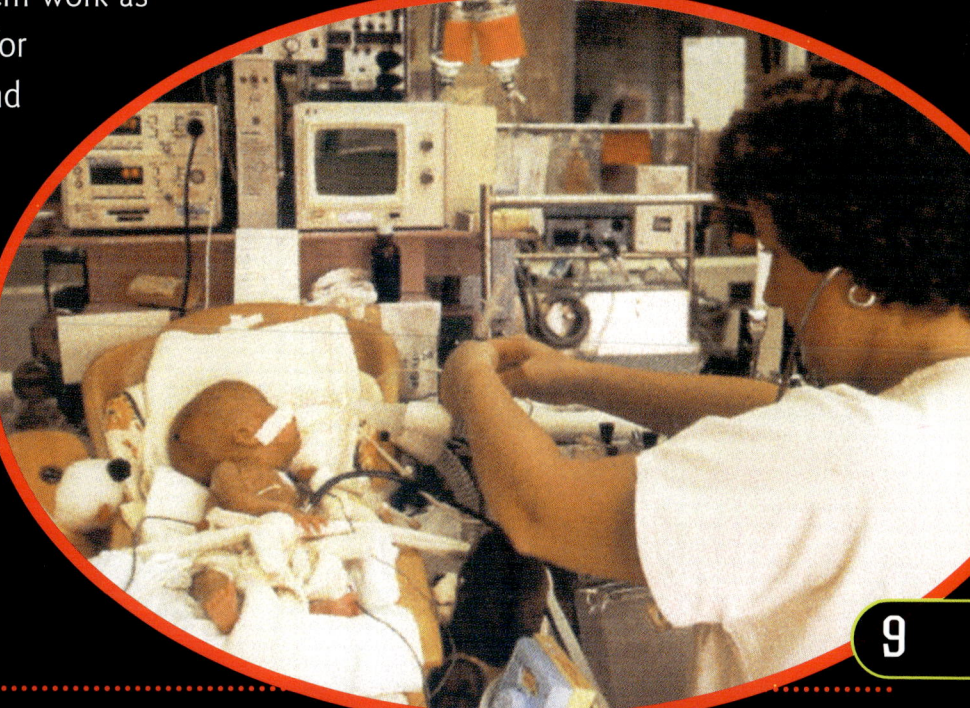

DIAGNOSIS

1900

New equipment

In 1900 doctors had new equipment to help with **diagnosis**. One of the biggest breakthroughs in diagnosis was in 1867, when French scientist, Louis Pasteur, proved that **germs** caused disease. This discovery was made with the help of newly improved microscopes that could give much greater magnification than earlier ones, so germs could be seen.

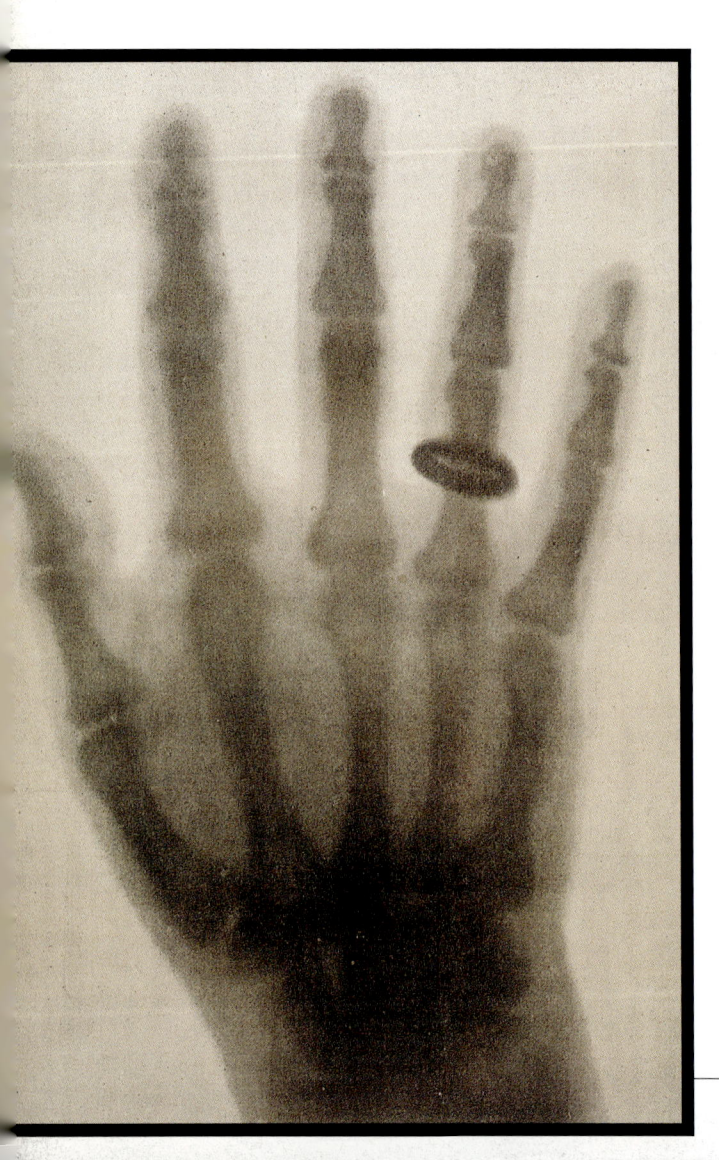

In 1895 Wilheim Roentgen discovered **X-rays**. This enabled surgeons to 'examine' a patient's insides without cutting them open. The less a patient was cut into, the less likely they were to get infected. In the same year the sphygmomanometer was invented to measure blood pressure. This told doctors if a patient had high blood pressure which made them more likely to have heart problems.

New techniques

Investigations were beginning into how blood was made up and how blood diseases could be found through tests and cured. In 1900 Karl Landsteiner, an Austrian scientist, discovered that there were different blood groups. This explained why blood **transfusions** had so often failed to work before – it was because blood of the wrong type was being transfused. He found the blood groups O, A, B and AB; the Rhesus groups were not discovered until 1939.

The first ever X-ray. It is the hand of Roentgen's wife. X-rays let you see bones and other hard objects in the body, such as gallstones.

2000

New equipment

There are now machines to measure almost every function of the body, from your heart beat to your lung capacity to the amount of **cholesterol** in your blood. Electron microscopes are now 30 times as powerful as the best microscopes in 1900 – they can show single cells from living things (the average cell measures 0.025 millimetres across).

X-rays were found to have health risks for patients, so they are now done as little as possible. Other forms of body scanning have been developed which let doctors see the soft parts of the body, as well as bones. **Ultrasound scanning** is used to examine the outside surface of organs (so it can be used to look for diseases of the liver, for example) and also babies in the womb (it can show how many babies there are, where they are lying and if they have any abnormalities). There are other kinds of scanners, too. **CAT scanners** use fine X-rays, which are less dangerous, to show up bone-related problems. **PET scanners** diagnose problems with the brain. **MRI scanners** scan the whole body, bones and soft tissue to build up a complete picture of the inside of a patient's body.

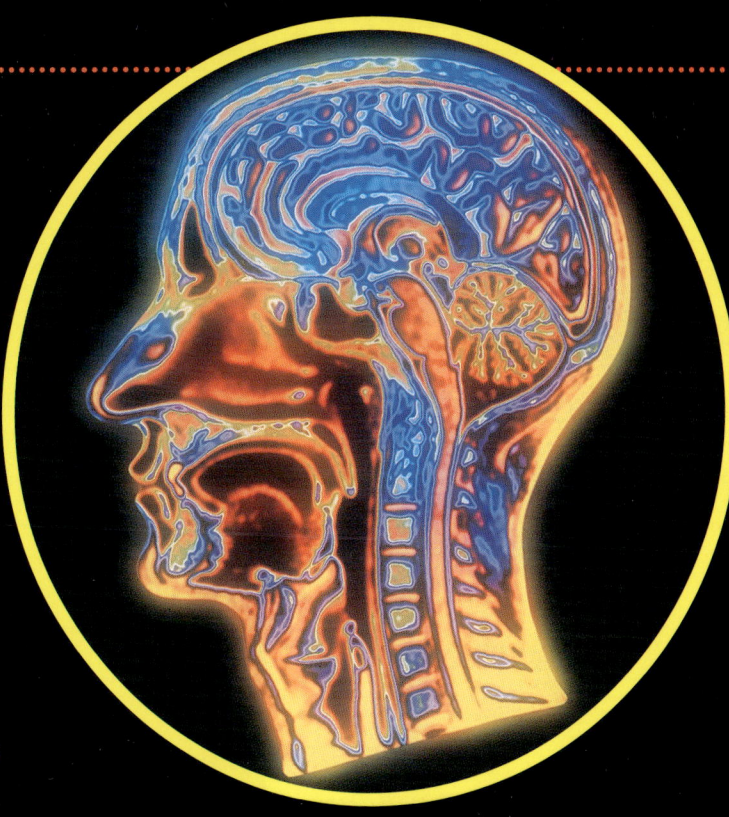

This is a MRI scan of a human head. You can see the soft tissue of the brain, and the spine.

New techniques

Computer technology helps doctors to perform many tests on blood and tissue to check for diseases such as leukaemia. The machines can do the tests in a matter of hours, and can detect a disease long before the physical signs are obvious.

Computers can be programmed to convert an MRI scan so that it can be looked at from different angles, and certain areas can be seen in close-up. The computer even allows doctors to try out various ways of doing an operation they want to perform.

HOSPITALS

1900

A cleaner, safer place

There were more hospitals in 1900 than ever before. Their doctors were trained, and many of their nurses were trained too. Hospitals were much cleaner than they had been 50 years before. Patients were no longer put into beds with sheets that were still dirty, or even bloody, from the previous patient. Patients were washed. Many doctors and nurses washed their hands after treating one patient before treating the next one. The wards were scrubbed regularly and kept clear of pests, such as rats.

Not all good

While hospitals were undoubtedly safer places in 1900 than they had been before, patients still only went to them as a last resort. Patients were more likely to survive a visit to hospital than they had been. But, even with improved **hygiene** and medical techniques, they still only had a 50 per cent chance of coming out alive.

The Children's Ward of the Royal Hospital, Portsmouth, photographed in 1902. The ward was designed to be as hygienic as possible. The beds are high, to make it easy to clean under them. The varnished floors and bare walls were scrubbed regularly. There is as little furniture in the ward as possible. You can just see, at the edge of the picture, a rocking horse for the children to play on. These and other shared toys were, like all toys at the time, made from wood and metal which were hard to keep germ-free. The metal was often lead and the paint lead-based: lead is poisonous.

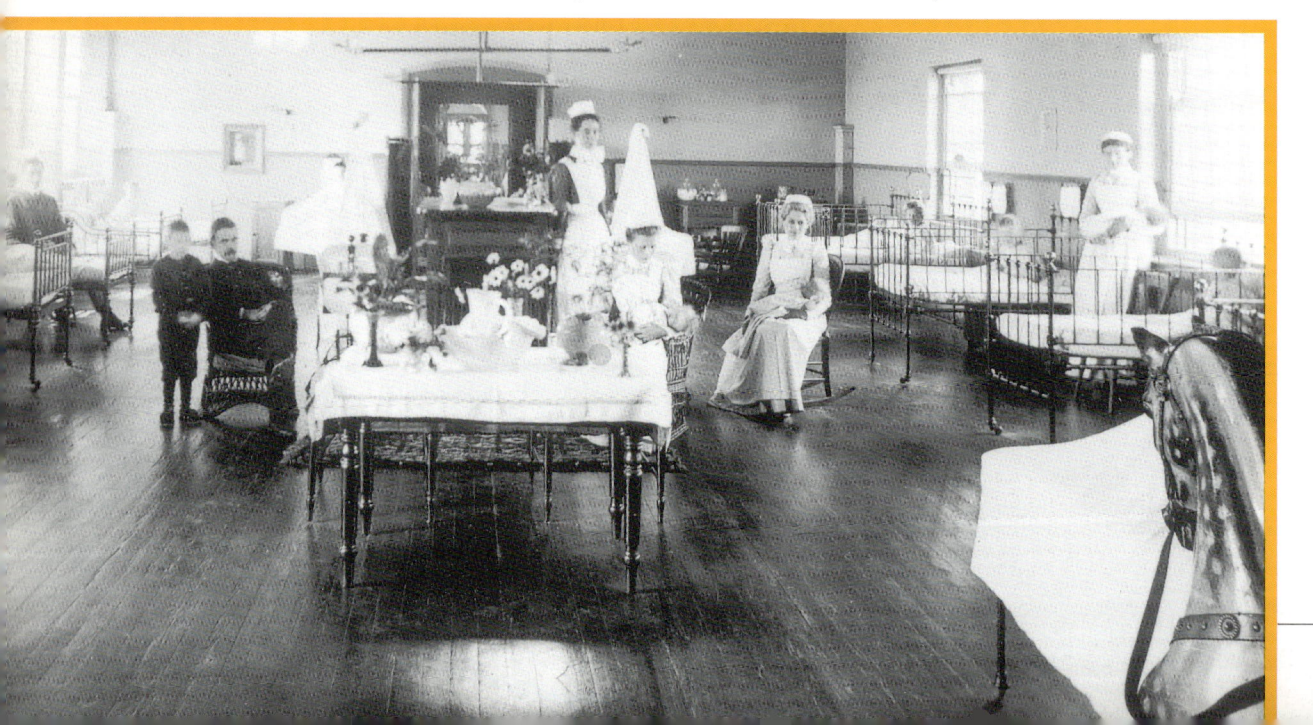

2000

Cleaner and safer?

Modern hospitals try to keep everything as clean as possible. The furniture is made of materials, such as stainless steel, which do not trap dirt and blood. Unclean surfaces would spread germs and cause infection, leading to fevers or even the death of patients. Hospital workers **sterilize** equipment to get rid of germs. Doctors and nurses sometimes wear very thin disposable gloves to examine patients; they wash their hands after examining each patient, using an **antiseptic** washing solution. They wear sterile clothes during operations, including disposable gloves.

Safe enough?

Although modern hospitals are safer than those in 1900, germs still persist. Germs adapt to the level of cleanliness in a hospital, changing so that they can resist antiseptics. Even in the best hospitals there are occasional outbreaks of infection which can spread rapidly from patient to patient, sometimes killing the weaker ones, just as they did in 1900.

Modern hospitals, like this one, can care for babies born early, who would not have lived had they been born in 1900. Babies can be born as many as twenty weeks early and still stand a chance of survival. These babies have problems with their breathing and other body functions – they have to be given time to grow as they would have done inside the womb. They are cared for in special wards of their own.

PAIN RELIEF

1900

Anaesthetics

Anaesthetics stop patients feeling pain during an operation. They either put them to sleep (a general anaesthetic) or stop the nerves in one part of their bodies from feeling anything (a local anaesthetic). Before anaesthetics, many patients died after an operation from pain and shock. Between 1845 and 1900, doctors tried various general anaesthetics. One of the greatest concerns was what dose to give – too large a dose could kill the patient, while too small a dose meant they still felt pain. By 1900, doctors were accurate about dosage, and some began to specialize as anaesthetists.

Antiseptics

In the past, if shock did not kill patients after operations, then the infections that set in usually did. From 1867 onwards more and more doctors used **carbolic acid** as an **antiseptic** to kill **germs**, a technique pioneered in Britain by Dr Robert Lister. When the operating theatre and the surgeon's hands and instruments were sprayed with the acid, deaths from infection fell by about 30 per cent. Some doctors and nurses refused to use the spray at first, because it irritated the skin of their hands. But by 1900, most hospitals were using antiseptics and improved **hygiene** to fight infection.

This is a photograph of Dr Boyd operating at Charing Cross Hospital in London in 1900. His patient has been anaesthetised.

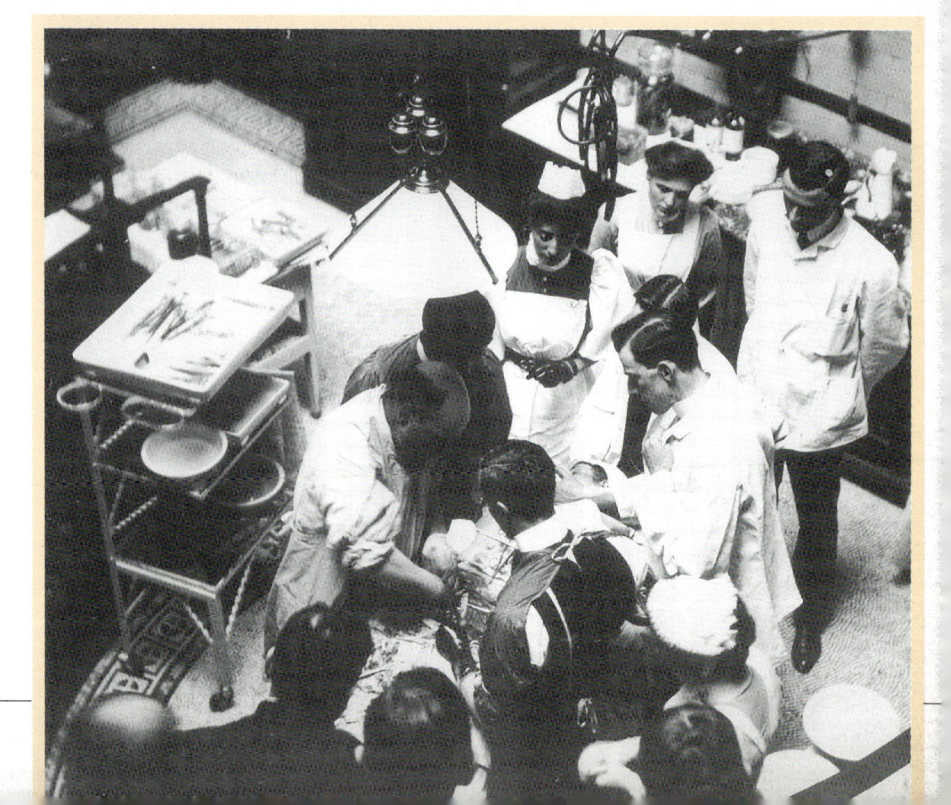

2000

Anaesthetics

Modern anaesthetists still use gas as a general anaesthetic. Too much of an anaesthetic can still kill a patient. Rather than use a huge dose to be certain of knocking the patient out, modern anaesthetists use a steady stream, just enough to keep the patient unconscious. They use local anaesthetics, too.

A new form of local anaesthetic, the epidural, allows the patient to stay conscious, but numbs feeling below the waist. It is injected into the patient's spine, between the vertebrae. It is especially useful during childbirth.

Antiseptics

It is as important to fight infection now, as it was in 1900, and almost as hard. New antiseptics have been developed that do not have the drawbacks of early carbolic acid, and they do not irritate the skins of doctors, nurses, or the patients. Most antiseptics today, such as TCP, have a carbolic acid base, but it has been mixed with other chemicals to make it kinder to the skin.

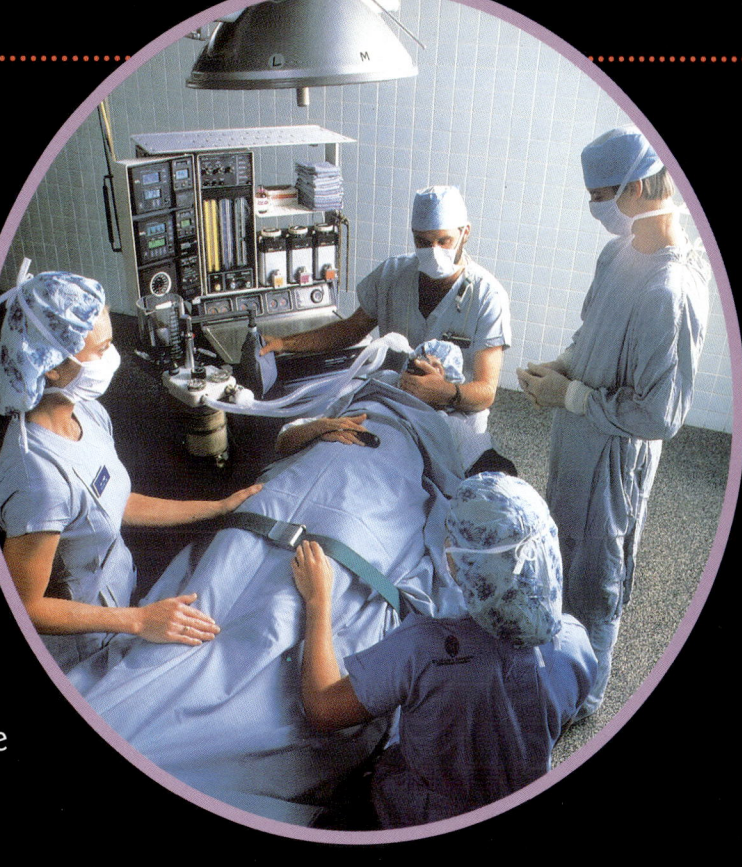

Modern anaesthetists have a lot of equipment to monitor the patient's condition. They have several kinds of anaesthetics to choose from, too.

Eastern anaesthetics move west

Traditional Chinese medicine uses **acupuncture** as an anaesthetic. Now, a western anaesthetic needs less training to administer than acupuncture. Less than half the operations performed in modern China use acupuncture as an anesthetic, due to the lack of trained staff. Acupuncture has been used successfully as an anaesthetic in western hospitals; but has met with too much distrust from both surgeons and patients to have come into general use yet.

SURGERY

1 9 0 0

Early surgery

Before 1800, surgeons had not understood the need for even basic **hygiene** in operations. They wore the same clothes every time they operated and put patients onto the same operating table without changing the sheets.

Surgery ... then

By the 1890s surgeons wore special clothes to operate in, which were washed after each operation. But only a very few doctors thought it was necessary to wear rubber gloves. Most just washed their hands before operating. Surgeons did not wear masks to stop them breathing **germs** onto the patient, either.

Surgeons now realized that they needed to wash their instruments before each operation, but did not **sterilize** them. Some surgeons used a **carbolic** spray while operating, to kill germs. By the turn of the century, operating conditions were cleaner than before, but the risk of infection was still high.

Not all surgeons accept change for the better. One surgeon, Lawson Tait, argued in 1882, that the use of carbolic spray was unnecessary. He said: '*I fill the abdomen with warm water and wash all the organs. The water is plain unfiltered tap water, and has not been boiled.*'

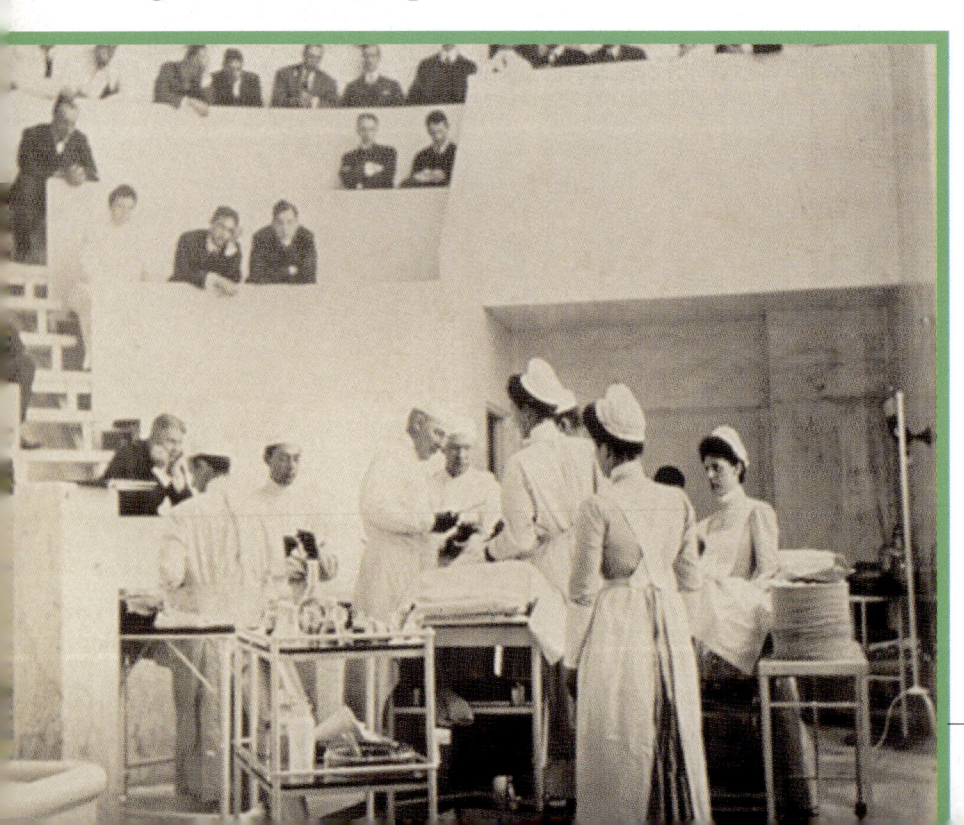

The students watching this operation are wearing ordinary clothes. They are not wearing masks. The operating theatre is far from sterile!

2000

Surgery ... now

Surgeons in the 1990s operate in a sterile environment. They wear gloves and masks, as do any students who are being taught in an operating theatre. Their instruments are sterilized. If they drop one they use another. They do not just pick it up and carry on, as earlier surgeons did! Surgeons also try to open up bodies as little as possible. New instruments and inventions help them to perform 'keyhole' surgery through a small cut, where surgeons can see what is happening inside the body on a special monitor. This reduces the shock to the patient and also reduces the risk of infection.

Heart operations

In the 1890s surgeons did not perform heart operations. If they tried, the patient died. During World War II a US army surgeon, Dwight Harken, operated on soldiers with bomb fragments in their hearts. His operations worked, but he found he had just four minutes before the interrupted flow of blood to the brain caused brain damage.

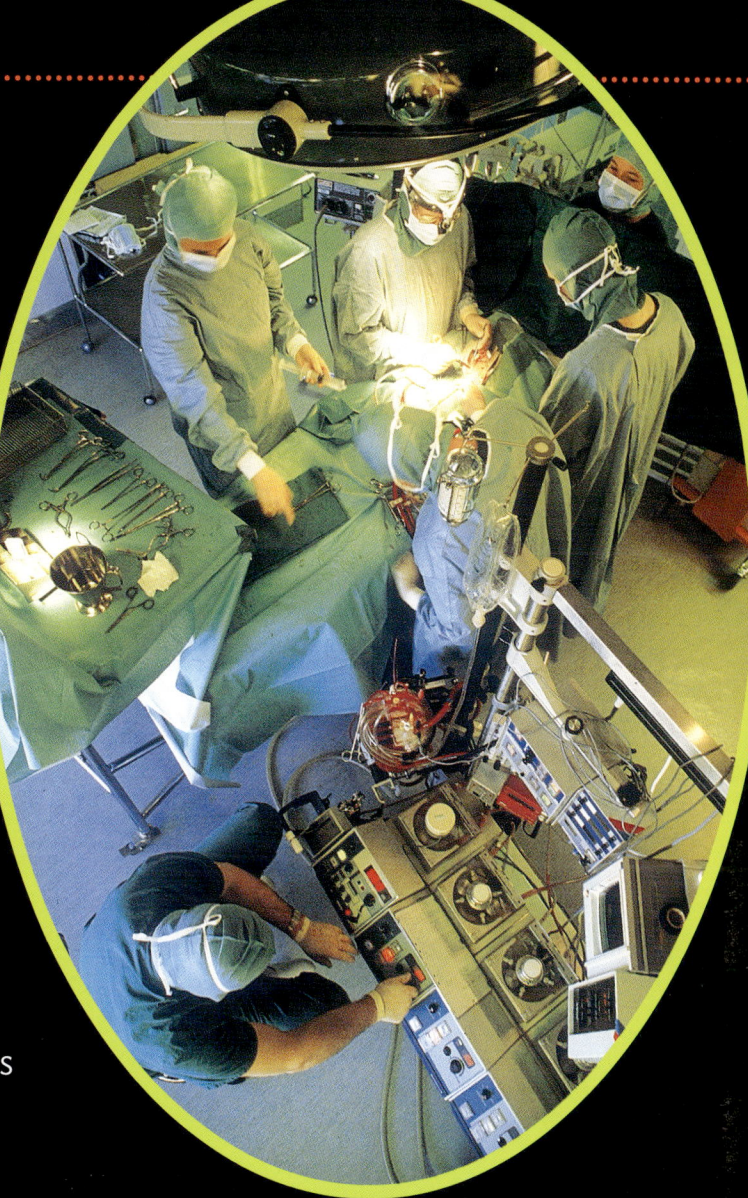

An operation in the 1990s. Notice all the machines to check on the state of the patient.

Surgeons then worked on lowering the temperature of the body to extend the operating time. Machines were invented to do the work of the heart during the operation. Now surgeons in the USA and Britain perform over 3000 heart operations every day.

17

KILLER DISEASES

1900

Almost defeated

In 1900 **developed countries** were celebrating the fact that they were definitely winning against the water-borne killer diseases – typhoid, cholera and dysentery. These diseases had been the biggest killers of the previous centuries. It is hard to estimate numbers as accurate records were not kept. They came in **epidemic** waves. The 1849 epidemic killed over 50,000 people in Britain, over 2,500,000 in Russia and 5000 in New York City alone. The provision of sewers, drains and piped water in towns and cities meant that sewage did not mix with drinking water. This greatly reduced heath risks, so epidemics in the early 1900s only affected hundreds, not thousands.

New discoveries

Infectious diseases like smallpox, diphtheria and tuberculosis were still killing people in large numbers. But scientists had discovered the link between **germs** and diseases like these and could isolate the germs to produce **vaccines** to kill them.

A vaccine that protected people from smallpox had been discovered in 1796, by Edward Jenner, an English doctor. At first people did not think his vaccine would work, but by 1850 there was enough evidence to convince most people that it did. By 1900, the numbers of deaths because of smallpox had sharply declined.

Even when cholera seemed to be under control, people still remembered it as a killer disease. This poster shows that people suspected of having cholera were not allowed into the USA.

2000

Back with a vengeance?

Water-borne diseases, like cholera, dysentery and typhoid, are now under control in the developed world. They still ravage **developing countries**, striking in areas where poor living conditions mean that sewage can pollute drinking water. Some people fear that they may re-appear in the developed world, if the conditions of the poor and homeless continue to get worse.

A rapid return

Tuberculosis (TB) was an airborne disease, known since medieval times, but killing most people in the 1860s. By 1950 a vaccine, discovered in 1906 but only slowly brought into use, had cut the number of deaths. The vaccine was then used as part of a WHO (World Health Organization) campaign in the developing world.

In the 1980s WHO was beginning to hope that TB had been virtually wiped out. However, a slowing in the vaccination programme has resulted in a rapid rise in TB cases. The number of new cases each year jumped from 7.5 million in 1990 to nearly 10 million in 1996.

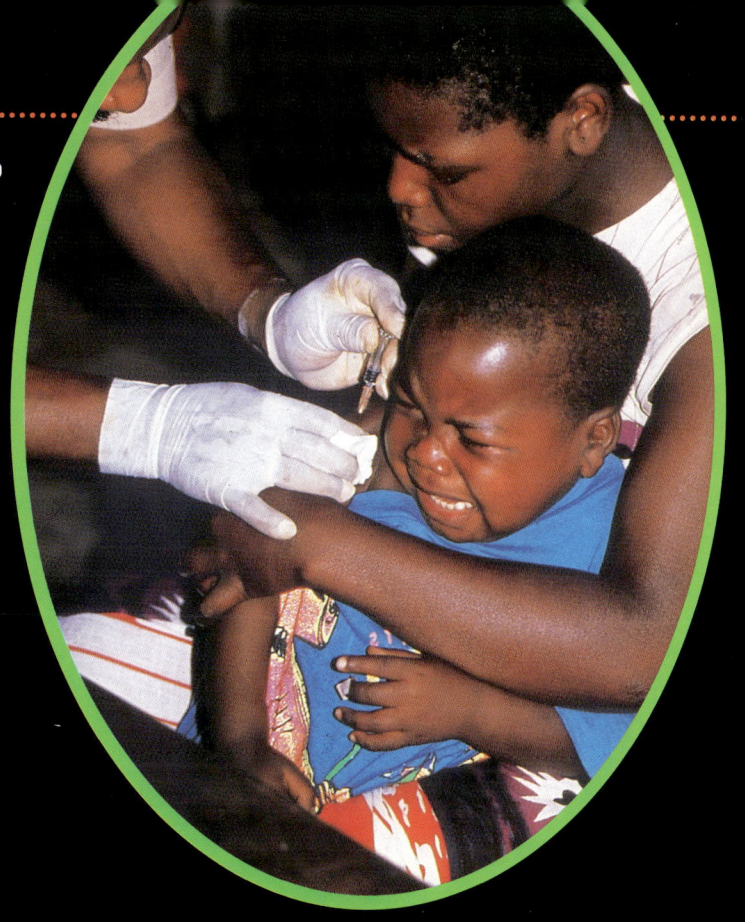

Only the vaccination of each generation keeps killer diseases away, otherwise they can reappear frighteningly quickly. This baby in Africa is being vaccinated against malaria.

New discoveries

Scientists are working on cures for the new killer diseases, such as cancer and heart disease. They are finding new links between **genes** and disease, just as people in 1900 were finding links between germs and disease. They have identified the genes that pass on **hereditary** diseases, such as cystic fibrosis. Scientists hope that infectious diseases, like influenza and TB, may be cured by changing people's genes to fight these infections.

MEDICINE

1900

The new drugs

The discovery of **germs** led to the search for a new sort of medicine – synthetic 'magic bullets' that kill germs without harming the rest of the body. By 1900 there was lots of research into drugs that would fight one or more of the newly discovered germs that caused killer diseases like cholera, dysentery and TB. People were sure they were close to a breakthrough. Much of the money for this research was given by new companies that sprung up to mass-produce the drugs, such as Burroughs and Wellcome and Co.

Mass-produced drugs

Relatively few medicines that cured disease were available. Instead there was a wide range of drugs to dull pain. Many of these, such as heroin and opium, were addictive. In 1900 aspirin, made with a chemical version of willow bark extract (which had been used as a painkiller for centuries), was just beginning to be used as a painkiller. Anyone who could afford the equipment and materials could make or sell drugs. From 1860 onwards, the development of machines that compressed ingredients into tiny pills and the development of gelatin capsules meant that pills could be mass-produced to make big profits.

This is a postcard of a pharmacy in Paris in 1900. On the windows are adverts for the products it sold.

2000

The drugs explosion

Since 1900, researchers have discovered an increasingly wide range of medicines. One of the biggest breakthroughs was the discovery of **antibiotics**, the 'magic bullets' that target germs. Unfortunately, germs are now becoming resistant to some antibiotics. Researchers also discovered steroids, drugs that change the **hormones** in the body. Steroids are used to treat blood disorders, such as clotting and anaemia. But steroids only work if they are taken regularly – they are not a cure. They can have quite severe side effects too, such as aggressive behaviour.

Scientists are beginning to experiment with ways to permanently change the **genes** in the body. Rather than trying to correct the problems caused by 'bad' genes that cause disease, doctors would add a 'good' gene to the body that would cancel out the effects of the 'bad' one. So, if they cancelled out the gene that produced anaemia there would be no need for steroids to counteract it.

Today's pharmacies stock a wide range of medicine. This pharmacist is completing a patient's prescription before she can dispense the medicine.

Careful regulation

Most countries now have laws about who can sell medicines. Some medicines can only be bought with a doctor's **prescription**. There are regulations about what goes into medicines, and regulations about the tests that have to be done before a new medicine goes on sale to the public, or is used by doctors.

1900

Dosing yourself

Because there were few useful medicines to cure disease, people often used traditional remedies, many of which worked. Herbal cures like chewing willow leaves as a painkiller is one example. But people were also lured into using remedies sold as medicines by people and drug companies that were not real cures at all. *Dr Giraud's Ginger Brandy*, for example, was sold in the USA as a certain cure for cholera, colic, cramps, dysentery, chills and fever. Most of these so-called medicines were harmless, but some were not.

By 1900 many people were pressing for government regulation of drug production and sale.

This advert for 'Eno's fruit salt' appeared in a London Newspaper in 1897. It claimed to be a 'simple precaution' against the 'jeopardy of life'.

Available medicines

Medical books in 1900 produced lists of various drugs. But, ignoring the drugs for controlling pain, the main curative medicines available to doctors were:
purgatives: to clear bowels
quinine: for malaria
mercury: used to treat ringworm
digitalis and amyl nitrate: used to treat various heart problems.

2000

Medicine today

One of the most noticeable changes made in medicine in the twentieth century is the development of new drugs. In the past the discovery of new drugs was largely down to chance. Today, millions of pounds are spent, usually by pharmaceutical companies, researching new drugs. The range of drugs available is therefore considerably more than in the 1900s.

A whole new market

In 1900 the average life expectancy in a **developed country** was 45 for men, 49 for women. By 1998 it had risen to 73 for men and 80 for women. Many women in these countries are having babies later in life and expect to stay fitter and younger looking for longer too. They are the main targets for companies that make various creams and pills which are supposed to slow down ageing.

There are many products available which claim to slow down the ageing process. The advert for this treatment for **hereditary** hair loss adopts the medically proven angle in an attempt to gain more sales.

If you suffer from hereditary hair loss, there's only one thing for it.

Mark Devine, Regaine user since April '96.

No one likes losing their hair, but hereditary hair loss is a common aspect of adult life. In fact it accounts for the majority of all hair loss.

If it doesn't worry you all well and good, but if it does we may be able to help. That's because Regaine is the only product medically proven for the treatment of hereditary hair loss and has been used by over 5 million men and women worldwide since 1988.

How does it work? It's likely that it increases the blood supply to hair follicles in the scalp, although nobody is absolutely sure.

In consumer surveys of over 7,000 male users more than 80% of them said they'd noticed the difference.

How do you use it? Regaine can easily be incorporated into a daily routine and only takes a few seconds to use. It should be applied twice a day by spraying or rubbing onto the affected areas of the scalp with a 12 hour interval between each application. Once you start it's important to stay committed because it may take 4 months for any improvement to appear. Any new hair could disappear if you stop in that time and the normal hair loss process will start again unless you keep using it.

What should you expect? After a few months, you may notice less hair in the sink or shower. A little later the new hair may be soft and downy, while later on it could change and become the same colour and thickness as the rest of your hair.

We can't predict how well it will work for each individual because not everyone will respond to Regaine in the same way, but we do know it's most effective in the early stages of hair loss.

Where can you buy it and what's the price? Regaine is available from your pharmacist without a prescription and costs £24.95 for 30 days' supply. As this works out at about 83p per day, and could help you keep your hair, its not such a great loss is it?

For more information, fill in the coupon or call 0345 004 500 or visit our website, www.regaine.co.uk

Always read the label. Contains minoxidil. Requires continuous use.

23

ALTERNATIVE MEDICINE 1900

Other cultures

In 1900 there were many cultures that had their own medical ideas that were distinct from 'western' medicine. In places as far apart as Africa and Hawaii people relied on a mixture of spiritual and herbal cures to treat illnesses that ranged from fevers to mental disorders. So, an infected wound would be covered with a herbal poultice to draw out the pus and infection. But this would not be expected to work unless particular prayers or chants were said as well. Chinese medicine was well-established and used a mixture of herbal and **homeopathic** drugs as well as **acupuncture**.

Other systems

In countries that relied mainly on western medicine, there were people ready to try new cures, especially as conventional medicine had so few medicines available. People tried hypnotism (then called mesmerism), homeopathy, faith healing and even doses of electricity as alternative cures for everything from headaches to giving up smoking.

This cartoon makes fun of the public perception of the cure-all effects of radium, discovered by Marie and Pierre Curie in 1898. Radium destroyed diseased cells and was eventually used to treat cancer.

LATEST CHRISTMAS NOVELTY.

2000

Other cultures

The twentieth century has seen many other cultures absorbed into western culture – together with alternative medical practices, such as reflexology and acupuncture. Most other cultures now use some of the elements of western medicine alongside their own. Many Chinese hospitals use conventional western medical practices, such as **anaesthetics** in surgery, as well as traditional Chinese methods, like acupuncture.

Acupuncture involves pushing special needles into the skin at certain points. There are hundreds of points, all over the body. When inserted at the right points the needles block pain so an operation can be performed on a conscious patient. In the early days of anaesthetics this had huge advantages because it avoided dosing problems.

Other ways

Alternative methods of healing, however, have become more widespread in **developed countries**, possibly as a reaction against the technology and drug-driven medical practice there.

More people are turning to alternative medical systems; many of which stress the need to live in the right way to be healthy. These systems, like the Alexander technique and homeopathy, advise about diet and lifestyle and offer cures that rely on herbs or physical manipulation rather than the use of machines and technology.

This shop has a section selling alternative and new era medicines.

25

Hydrotherapy

Hydrotherapy was very popular in 1900. People went to stay in spas – places that had natural water springs, often with a high mineral content. The theory was that the water would 'purify the system' removing all the unhealthy elements in the body. People drank the water and gargled it. They took hot and cold baths, and were wrapped in wet bandages. In some places they were even told they had to sleep in wet sheets! Because it was fashionable, and many of the people who went to spas were rich people, who drank and ate too much and exercised too little, spas often had a good effect, if only temporarily.

Allier — 206 - VICHY, le Gargarisme

This is a postcard from Vichy Spa in France. You can see people gargling with the water found there. They are in a special room called a 'Gargarisme'.

The alkaline water found at Vichy was thought to be able to get rid of any impurities in the body, especially in the bowels.

2000

Flowing energy

One idea that is becoming popular world-wide is that our bodies carry energy, as well as blood, that this energy needs to flow freely around the body, just as blood does. Any blockages in the flow of energy make the patient ill. **Acupuncture**, acupressure and reflexology all try to get the patient's energy moving freely.

Many people also believe that energy needs to flow freely in their homes and offices. They apply the system of *feng shui* to the design and arrangement of these places. *Feng shui* experts say that properly arranged homes and offices keep energy flowing and keep the people in them healthy, wealthy and happy.

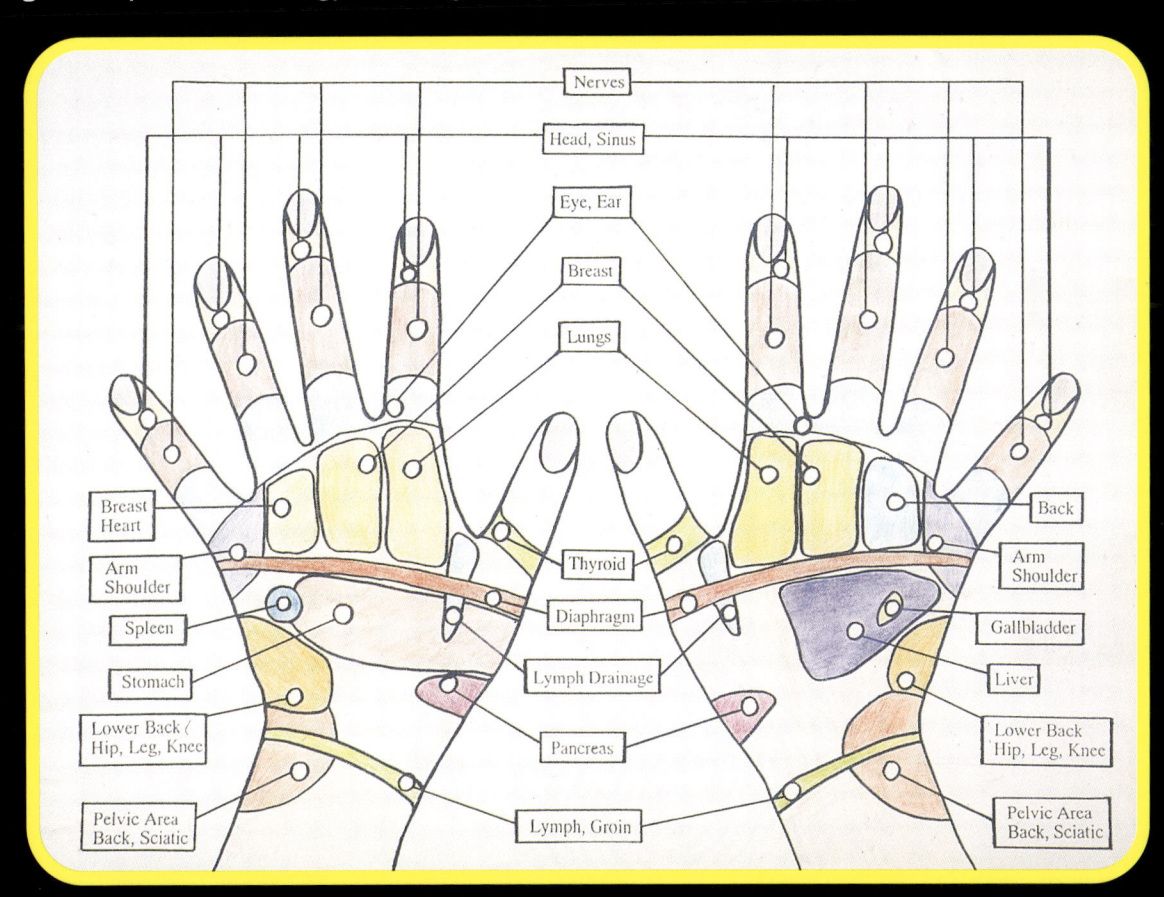

This reflexology chart shows areas of the hand that are affected by different parts of the body. For example, the fingertips are affected by the head and sinus. Reflexology came from 'zone theory' which was developed in the USA in the early 1900s. This theory states that the body is divided into ten areas running from the feet to the head and back down to the hands, passing through organs. Pain in a particular area of the hand relates to a problem in the corresponding organ. Massaging the correct area of the hand is supposed to treat the problemed organ.

27

THE FUTURE?

In the 21st century the most important **diagnosis** and treatment advances will be made by using **molecular medicine**. Molecular medicine uses **DNA** analysis to break down **viruses** and find out how to beat them. So how will doctors find out what is wrong with us in the future?

Molecular medicine will also be able to track down and beat cancers and **hereditary** diseases. Many people think that, in the future, there will not be a single sort of medicine or cure for a disease. How you are treated will depend, to a large extent, on your own personal genetic makeup.

Changing genes

William R. Clarke, Professor of Immunology at UCLA, says in his book *The New Healers*, that **gene** research will reach the point where diseases can be cured by implanting genes: *'Having survived the attack of viral disease, we will still have to fight genetic disease. Already, we can isolate human genes, copy them in the laboratory and give them to people with 'bad' genes – they take over the function of the 'bad' gene. In future, we could introduce carefully controlled 'bad' genes to attack and destroy unwanted cells – for instance cells infected with cancer and AIDS.'*

This is a computer graphic of human DNA. Everybody has a different DNA structure.

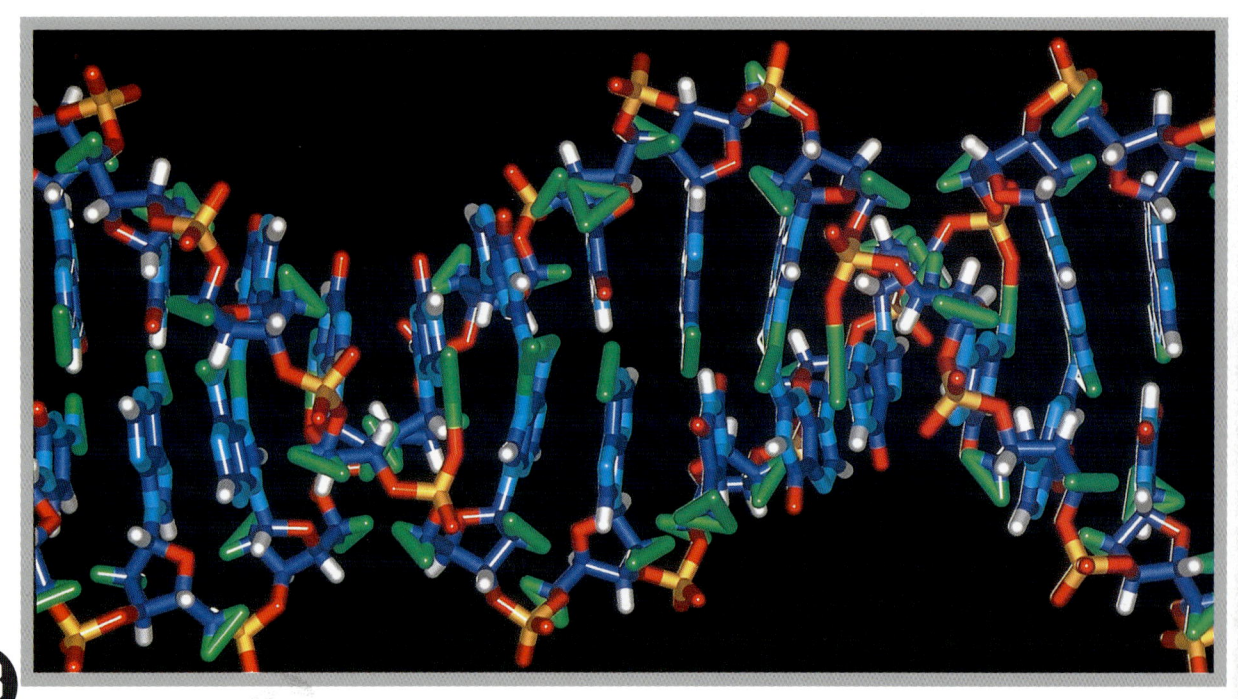

We will be able to design more than just our environment. Doctors in the future will be able to alter babies' genes to avoid genetic disease. They may be able to breed babies outside the womb. This poses problems. Arthur Caplan of the University of Pennsylvania Centre for Bioethics says in *Visions*: '*this is the greatest moral challenge we will ever face. We need to decide to what extent we want to design our descendants*'.

Some of the problems

William R. Clarke, author of *The New Healers*, says that there are problems with making a person's 'gene map'.

'*The information provided by genetic testing can be used to prevent defects in babies. But will future parents demand that they scan the catalogue of all human genes, shopping for gene variants they would like to see in their children?*'

Problems with cloning

Just a few examples of possible problems with **cloning**, produced by Michio Kaku, Physics Professor at the city University of New York in his book *Visions*:

- dictators could clone themselves strong, completely obedient armies
- famous people's graves could be raided for DNA to clone them
- a 'black market' in cloning could spring up; so any rules set up to control cloning could be broken.

In 1997 scientists in Edinburgh, Scotland cloned the world's first sheep from an adult sheep cell. This is a picture of Dolly when she was eight months old.

GLOSSARY

acupuncture treating a patient by inserting needles into special points on the body

anaesthetic a drug that makes the patient unconscious, or numb in a certain part of the body

anatomy the study of how the body is put together

antibiotics drugs that kill germs inside the body

antiseptics things that kill germs outside the body

carbolic acid a weak acid, one of the first known antiseptics

CAT scan a computerized scan of the bones in the body

cholesterol a fatty substance that can clog the blood

clone an exact replica; produced by copying its genes

contagious easily spread from one person to another

developed/developing countries developed countries (such as the USA) are rich, industrial countries. Developing countries are began industrialization later.

diagnosis finding out what the disease is by studying the symptoms

DNA see gene

endoscope a medical instrument that is put into the body. It uses fibre optics to light up the insides of the body and reflect an image back onto an eyepiece.

epidemic a severe outbreak of a disease at a particular time

gallstones hard, painful stones that form in the gall bladder

gene (DNA) a body's genes tell you what a person will be like – the colour of their hair, their height, if they will have a particular disease

germ a small living bacteria which breeds in the body and causes disease

hereditary passed on through families from one generation to the next

homeopathy medicines that give the body small doses of various diseases to help the body become immune

hormones the substances in your body that affect your sex and how your body processes certain things, such as fats

hygiene keeping things clean

infectious see contagious

midwives people trained to look after pregnant women before and during the birth, and for a while after the baby is born

molecular medicine medicine that is concerned mainly with using genes to fight disease

MRI scan a magnetic scan of the soft tissue in the body

PET scan a scan which examines one of many substances in the body, such as blood. It can be used to study how blood flow changes in the body under different conditions

prescription a form from the doctor to the pharmacist telling what medicine to give a patient

specialize to study one particular area of a subject

sterilize to heat something so much it kills any germs

transfusion blood given to a patient to replace blood they have lost or diseased blood

ultrasound scan a scan that uses sound waves to form a picture of the soft tissue inside

vaccination a small dose of a disease, given so that the body can learn how to deal with that disease

virus a germ-like bacteria that is unaffected by antibiotics

X-rays rays that pass through the soft tissue to show the bones in the body. X-rays can harm the body if used too often.

INDEX

alternative medicine   4, 24, 25, 26, 27
anaesthetics   4, 14, 15, 25
antibiotics   5, 7
antiseptics   13, 14, 15, 16
Chinese medicine   6, 15, 24, 25
death rates   5, 8, 14, 18, 19
diagnosis   5, 10, 11, 28
emergency care   4, 8, 9, 13
germs   10, 13, 14, 16, 18, 20, 21
home visits   4, 6, 7
hospitals   4, 6, 7, 8, 9, 12, 13, 14, 15, 16, 17
hygiene   5, 8, 12, 14, 16, 17, 18, 19
infectious diseases   5, 6, 13, 18, 19, 20
Jenner, Edward   18
Landsteiner, Karl   10
Lister, Robert   10
medical machinery   5, 7, 9, 10, 11, 13, 17, 25
medicines   4, 5, 20, 21, 22, 23
midwives   4, 9
molecular medicine   5, 21, 26
NHS   5
Nightingale, Florence   8
operations   5, 8, 11, 14, 15, 16, 17, 25
Pasteur, Louis   10
payment for care   4, 5, 6, 7
prescriptions   5, 6, 21
Roentgen, Wilheim   10
specialization   9, 14
traditional remedies   4, 6, 22, 23
training   4, 8, 9
vaccination   4, 5, 18, 19
wars   8, 9, 17
water-borne diseases   18, 19, 20